Kiki

The Making of a School Therapy Dog

Diane Gilbert

PAGE PUBLISHING
Conneaut Lake, PA

First originally published by Page Publishing 2024

ISBN 979-8-89315-079-7 (pbk)
ISBN 979-8-89553-288-1 (hc)
ISBN 979-8-89315-109-1 (digital)

Printed in the United States of America

Dedication to Kiki

This dedication is to my amazing and precious Kiki who passed from our world and journeyed across the rainbow bridge. Her unconditional love, dedication, kind soul, and amazing personality will forever live in our hearts and in the hearts of those who were fortunate to meet her. Kiki was always giving of herself in innumerable ways. As a therapy dog, she helped countless students and many people who interacted with Kiki get through troubling days or just put a smile on their faces. Everyone who knew Kiki loved Kiki and she loved them right back. She was the district's first therapy dog. Today there are 19 therapy dogs spread throughout the district. Their work is a testimony to Kiki's legacy. They are continuing the amazing work of therapy dogs everywhere. We hope this story continues her legacy in some small way.

As our family member, she showed her love and personality in countless ways. She led by example, teaching all of us to be more patient. Kiki never complained about her brother Finnegan's shenanigans and just patiently worked around them. If Finn whined, she would come right over to make sure he was okay. She constantly showed us love and affection and one of her favorite spots was to sit next to you on the top step of our deck or our porch. On walks, if we weren't walking in the direction she preferred, she would stop in her tracks, refusing to move, take hold of the leash in her mouth, and lead us in the "right" direction. She let us know what she wanted by relentlessly looking back and forth from an object to us until we got the message. Whenever we came home, she wiggled her tail back and forth so fast that it seemed to travel in a circular motion. Not a day goes by that we don't miss her. We look forward to seeing Kiki again someday along with her warm tail-wagging greeting that we miss so much.

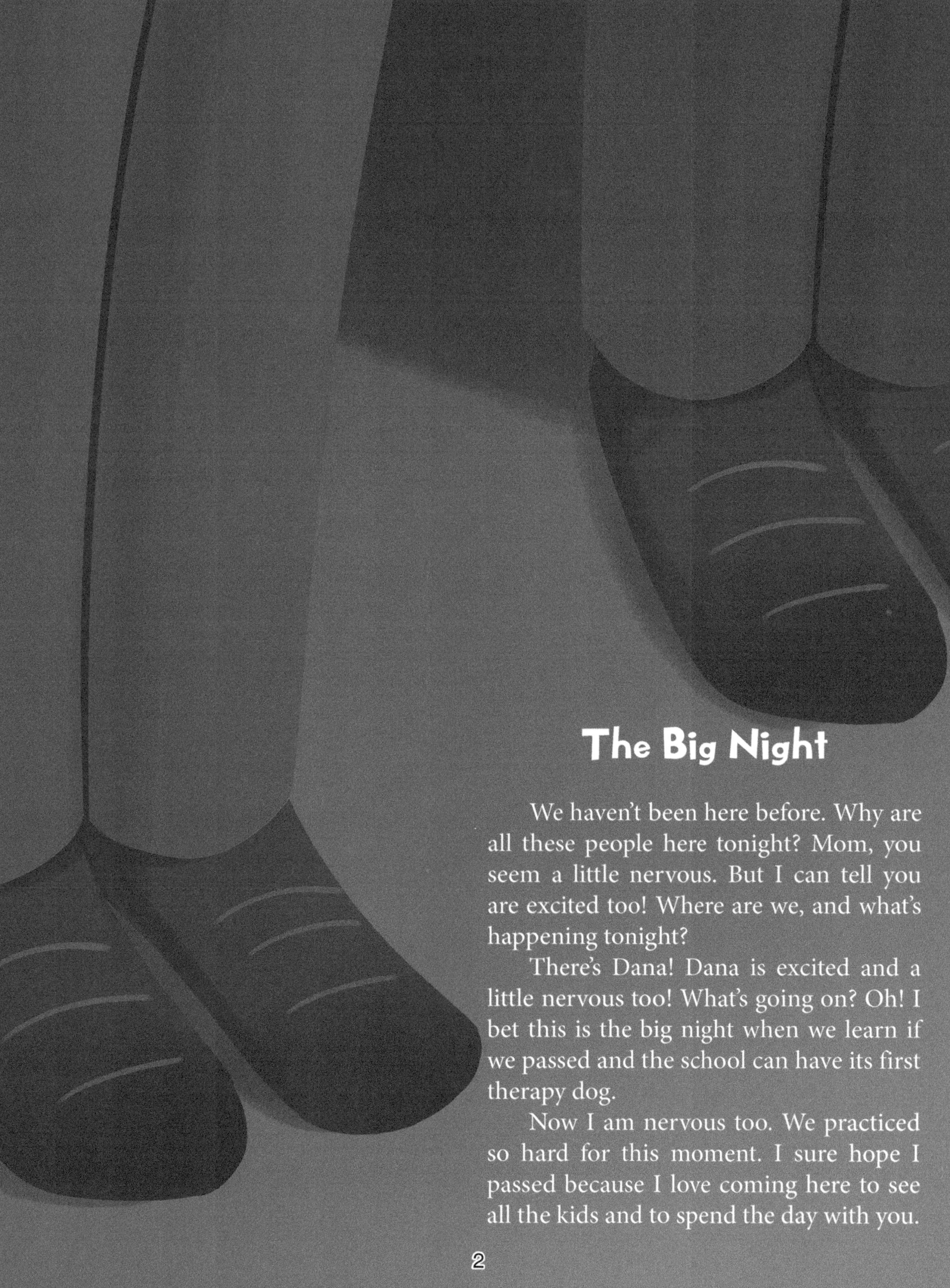

The Big Night

We haven't been here before. Why are all these people here tonight? Mom, you seem a little nervous. But I can tell you are excited too! Where are we, and what's happening tonight?

There's Dana! Dana is excited and a little nervous too! What's going on? Oh! I bet this is the big night when we learn if we passed and the school can have its first therapy dog.

Now I am nervous too. We practiced so hard for this moment. I sure hope I passed because I love coming here to see all the kids and to spend the day with you.

Kiki Goes to Dog Training School

Oh boy! Mom has my leash!
"Come, Kiki. Let's go," she says. I love "Let's go!"
Are we going for a walk? Are we going to the park? Are we going somewhere new?
I wonder where we are going. I am so excited my tail cannot stop wiggling!
Woohoo! We are at Justin's and Carrie's place. I can't wait to play with my friends.

Is today bring-your-mom-to-work day? Are you staying and playing with me? Are we meeting all the other parents?

Mom and I have been practicing so many tricks that we have learned in class such as sit, stay, leave it, heel, walking past a stranger and their dog, and much more. Mom is always happy and gives me treats when I do the tricks right.

I also learn how to greet new people with Mom by my side. It's best if we politely sniff human paws and then let people pet me under my chin. Sometimes humans aren't the best greeters because they try to pat me on the head before I sniff their paw. I don't like it when people reach for my head because I cannot see what their paws are going to do. So Mom and I show them how to greet me a better way. This makes me feel much more comfortable.

When we walk together, I follow Mom and stay by her side. I sit and wait patiently while she greets her friend. Sometimes her friend has a dog too, and we patiently sit or lie down and wait while they greet each other and talk. Another hard trick is staying when Mom leaves without me. I must sit quietly with my family or friends until she comes back. It seems like forever to me, but she always comes back with a smile and lots of pats. She says, "Hi, Kiki, I missed you!" and "Good job." I love pats and when she says, "Good job!"

Kiki Overcomes Her Fears

I was just having a good snooze when I saw that Mom has my leash again. It must be time for another adventure. Mom says, "Come on, Kiki, let's go. We are going to do some more training and practice today."

I love when she says, "Let's go."

But I wonder what "practice" means.

We are at one of my favorite places, the park, and we are practicing the tricks Justin taught us. A man is walking towards us, and he looks awfully scary to me. I cannot see his eyes, and he is wearing a strange thing on his head. I am so scared! I am not sure of that person. I say, "Mom, Wait! I will protect you!"

Mom pets me and says, "It's okay, Kiki. Don't be scared."

The man kneels, and he takes off his sunglasses and his cap. He lets me smell his glasses and his hat. He is talking to me in a kind, gentle way, and he is petting me nicely. I guess the strange things he was wearing aren't so scary after all.

The nice man puts the thing that covers his eyes back on and keeps talking to me while petting me. Next, he puts the thing on his head back on.

Oh, I get it! He's the same kind person with all those things on, and those things are just what people like to wear. It's just like I love to wear my special collar that has my name on it. I guess I'm not scared anymore.

"Watch out! Someone is running at us! He might run us over!"

Mom says, "It's okay, Kiki. Don't bark." I look at Mom, and she has that calm, "no worries" look on her face. I look back at the jogger, and he just keeps running right past us.

"Phew, that was a close one."

"Oh no! Here comes a whole pack of those running people! Oh, I get in it now. They are just having fun by chasing each other. Mom is right. There is nothing to worry about."

We also practice at other places and with other people so I would not be nervous or anxious with people and things that I might see.

Training School Test Day Arrives

Mom is filling the bath today. That can only mean one thing—it's bath time, and I hate bath time!

Don't tell me that you are going to brush my teeth again! Boy, this night cannot get any worse.

Mom says, "You'll look beautiful for your test tomorrow."

"What's a test? No one said anything about a test!"

The next morning, Mom and I go for a walk and then we practice all the skills we learned in front of our house. Afterward, Mom says it's test time, and we get into the car. Mom drives us to Justin's place. She smiles at me and pets me while saying, "You have worked so hard, and I am very proud of you. I know you will try your best, and that's all anyone can ask. But I also know you've got this, so let's go show them what you can do!"

We enter the testing room and go through the skills test. The lady told Mom and me that I passed her test. Everyone is so happy, and they are congratulating Mom and me. Mom and others are petting me, and they are so excited. Carrie kneels in front of me, and she is petting me. She is so happy, and she says, "Kiki, you did it! I am so proud of you!"

I am so excited. I wag my tail so hard!

Exploring the School

Before everyone comes back to school in September, Mom and I are going to her school so we can explore it together. Her friends, Dana and Scott, are meeting us there with his dog named Charlie. We are walking around the school exploring different things. We go up and down the stairs, we ride in elevators, we walk on different types of flooring such as tiling and nonslip strips. The tile floors are slippery, but I am learning how to walk on them without slipping. We explore the auditorium, which has a strange hill for a floor and connecting seats. We go into classrooms with a lot of strange things like noisy desks and chairs.

After exploring the inside of the school, we explore outdoor places like sidewalks, grassy fields, and tennis courts. There were a lot of new smells to explore. We had a great time. Let's do this again.

Opening Day of School

Mom and I are taking another trip to her school today. The parking lot is full of cars. It wasn't this way when we went to Mom's school before. What is going on today?

Mom and I walk to the big area in front of the room with the slanted floor and many rows of seats. There are so many people saying hello to each other. I'm a little unsure about all this, but Mom says everything is okay, and she introduces me to people who want to meet me and pet me. They are all very nice and happy to see me.

There's someone I know! It's Dana! "Hi, Dana! It's so good to see a familiar friend."

Dana says, "Hi, Kiki, let's go meet friends of mine."

Soon, all the people start walking into the auditorium. Dana, Mom, and I follow everyone. Everyone is looking for a seat, and we find a seat next to an aisle so I can lie down. Mom says that if I want, I can sit in her lap instead of lying on the floor. Soon everyone quiets down while a person talks into something that makes his voice *very* loud. I make sure to be quiet so everyone can hear him talk. While he is talking, I think I'll take a nap.

Wait. What did I miss? Did I hear my name mentioned? The loud talker said my name and something about the school's first therapy dog. What's going on? Why is everyone standing and clapping their paws? Is that for me?

After we leave the auditorium, Mom and I go to something called a "meeting." She introduces me to people who want to meet me. Then everyone gets to work. I lie down and take a nap in the meetings while everyone works. After the meeting, Mom and I go for walks both inside the school and outside the school whenever I need a break. Our friend Dana also comes to take me for walks and to introduce me to people. I really love the walks we take.

Mom says that it's time to go home. It has been a long and busy day. I've met so many nice people and experienced so many new things. I am very tired, and I'm very glad that it's time to go home. I think I'll take another nap on the way home.

First Day of Classes

Mom takes me to work again, and there are so many more people. They may be smaller than the people I met before, but they are *much* louder. The principal and I greet the students as they get off the big yellow buses and make their way into the school. Many of the students are making funny sounds and saying things like "Aww," "There's a dog!" "Can I pet the dog?" and "What's its name?"

Kids reach out and try to pat me on my head at first. Mom is right there to teach them how I prefer to meet people. I like to sniff their paw first and then I like them to scratch my chin. Now I know they are my friends, and it is safe to let them pet me.

Almost all the students are off the bus, so Mom and I make our way to her classroom. Bells ring, and Mom says it's time to go into her classroom and meet the class. She introduces me and explains that I am the school's first pilot therapy dog. My job is to make their day a little brighter and to help them when they are feeling sad, stressed, lonely, in need of a break, or for any other reason. Even if it just puts a smile on their face when they see me or pet me. Mom tells the students they don't have to interact with me if they prefer not to. No one will judge them poorly because dogs aren't for everyone, and it's perfectly okay. She asks if anyone is allergic to dogs or scared of dogs so she can plan for me to visit our friend Dana during their class period.

My School Days

When I come to school with Mom, we say hello to Dana and our other friends. The principal takes me to greet the students at the bus drop off. Someone brings me back to Mom's room, and as we make our way there, we meet and greet students in the hall before class begins. In the hallways and in class, I hear the kids say things like "She's so soft!" "This made my day!" "Can I come back later to see her?" "It's just amazing how much better I feel after just a few minutes with Kiki," "She's so calming," and "I love Kiki."

I am so glad that I can rest when I need to rest because sometimes spending time with so many kids can tire me out. Kids have a lot of energy, and sometimes they feel a lot of different feelings. They may be happy or sad, relaxed, concerned, excited, tired, or other things. I can feel their energy level and how they are feeling. I try my best to comfort them when they need comfort, play with them when they want to play, or just sit by them and let them pet me.

Spending a lot of time with kids can tire me out, and I need time to rest. So Mom set up a quiet space with a water bowl, a bed, toys, treats, and dog bubbles in her room. When I need alone time or I am tired or need a nap, then I just play with the

toys or I lie down in my bed and rest. Dana also has a bed, toys, snacks, and a water bowl in her office. Sometimes she comes to get me when I would like quiet time of my own.

During Mom's breaks, we go for a walk around the school and play with my toys. But if Mom is super busy, Dana or her friends take me out. I am so thankful to have Mom and her friends play with me, go for walks, or to let me rest with them. I love my time with Mom and our friends.

There are times when I must ask Mom to go outside during her class. It's like when students need a break, and they ask Mom to leave for a few minutes. Other times I make a special visit to the guidance office because someone needs my company. Dana takes me to visit other classes for special events or lessons. During these times, either Dana or another friend comes to pick me up. I am so happy that there are people around to help us.

Sometimes we make special visits to other schools too.

It is the end of the day, and boy, I am tired. Mom says that it is time to go home. I grab my leash in my mouth and lead Mom to the car. I know where Mom parked the car, and I don't want her to get lost. "C'mon, Mom! Follow me. I know the way! Walk faster because I'm tired!"

Dress-Up Days

Mom says today is another dress-up day. The school has many dress-up days for the students every year. I wear outfits that match a day's theme.

I dress up for Halloween, Homecoming Week, Pajama Day, St. Patrick's day, Valentine's Day, and other days too. The kids really like it when I wear special clothes for them.

We Did It!

We have all worked so hard this year. Mom says it's time to go in, find seats, and make our plea to the school board. First, Dr. Kilmer and then Dana are going to speak to the board. Mom says that all I need to do is sit on her lap and look pretty. I think that I can do that okay.

Boy, I am getting so nervous. I wish Dr. Kilmer and Dana would speak faster. I don't think I can stand it! I remember when we first came to school, and I was so nervous. I sure hope they approve, and we are no longer just a trial program.

The school board is now discussing it. Please, please say we passed! Oh boy! They passed us, they passed us!

I am officially a school therapy dog. Yippee!

Epilogue

I continued to come to school with Mom for two years before retiring. In that time, two more dogs became therapy dogs and my friends in the high school. During the two years, several more dogs were either in training to become school therapy dogs or they were already working therapy dogs in other schools within the district. To date, there are now nineteen therapy dogs in the district. They are making their way into the hearts and minds of students, faculty, and staff. They supply support to students who are having a bad moment, day, week, or more. They help students struggling with emotional needs and traumatic situations. I cannot imagine a school without a therapy dog. Each one is changing the lives of countless people.

Acknowledgments

So many people made all this possible. I cannot express adequately how much they had a positive effect on countless lives through their hard work and mentorship. They contributed, in so many countless ways, to the success of this program. I want to especially thank the following people in no particular order.

To begin, thank you Justin Bonn, Carrie Lindley, and Danielle of Justin's Canine Campus. Justin and Carrie, I have endless gratitude for the countless hours of support through training and mentoring you provided. Your pep talks and advice kept my spirits and confidence high. You always made yourselves available for consultations, and your advice was always spot on. Your intuition and guidance are amazing. I am truly grateful for your unselfish time and support for this program, Kiki and me, and for other pet owners and their dogs who have come to you. You are truly amazing. Danielle, thank you for all your advice. Whenever I asked for your thoughts, you were so great and always supplied such positive suggestions and feedback. You are amazing. It has been my absolute pleasure to meet and collaborate with all of you.

Dana, I don't even know where to begin. You were then and are now the backbone of the school's program. Without your research into several other schools' therapy dog programs, your advocacy for the need and benefits of such a program, for proposing the program to the school board, your willingness to give up your valuable time to train and the work out the logistics of a therapy dog program within the district's schools, and your love of students and their mental health and emotional needs, this program would not have been possible. Without your hard work and devotion to this program, so many lives would not have been so profoundly enriched by a dog's unconditional love and acceptance. Your willingness to go above and beyond to train with all the dogs and their handlers amazes me each and every time I think of it.

Heidi, who was a partner with Dana and all the handlers to create a Therapy Dog Program District Policy, I thank you so much. Your endless hours collaborating and researching the best policy for our district. Your partnership with Dana as a dog handler, when dogs are needed elsewhere or they just need a break, is so greatly appreciated. Your willingness to train and share Milo with us is so heartwarming and appreciated. Thank you for everything you do.

I thank my family for their support. Your time helping with the training at home or at the mall, visiting stores, and getting her comfortable with crutches, wheelchairs, and various other medical devices was priceless. Your training support and encouragement to write this book were amazing. I couldn't have done it without you.

I thank all the other dog parents and their therapy dogs. Their dedication and their contributions to their school and its students cannot be expressed adequately or underestimated. The dogs and their moms and dads help fulfill students' lives with such a positive and comforting experiences. Especially in times when students may need it the most. You are changing lives and making a difference.

Lastly, I would like to thank Fayetteville-Manlius' board of education for your support and recognition of the benefits of therapy dogs within the district. These times are so full of mental and emotional challenges. Your willingness to support this program cannot go without due recognition and gratitude. You took a chance on us, and I am so grateful. I can say, with fair certainty from my daily experiences with students and faculty, that you made the right decision. Thank you for all that you do.

About the Author

Diane Gilbert taught mathematics or computer science programming for thirty years at the high school level. In 2022, she retired from teaching.

She lives in Central New York with her husband of thirty-five years. It is also where they raised their two children. She enjoys many different craft hobbies, and she loves to visit Maine in the summer.